500-Calorie Delights

A Healthy and Tasty Recipe Collection

Elias Wolfe

Table of the Contents

Introduction

Welcome to our low-calorie recipe book! In this collection, you'll find delicious and satisfying dishes, all under 500 calories. Whether you're watching your weight, following a healthy lifestyle, or simply looking for lighter meal options, you'll find something to love here. Each recipe is carefully crafted to be packed with flavor, yet low in calories, so you can enjoy your food without sacrificing taste. So, let's get cooking!

Breakfast

Berry Yogurt Parfait

Ingredients:

- 1 cup Greek yogurt
- 1 cup mixed berries (strawberries, blueberries, raspberries, etc.)
- 2 tbsp honey
- 2 tbsp granola

Instructions:

1. In a clear glass, layer half of the Greek yogurt.
2. Top with half of the mixed berries.
3. Repeat the layers with the remaining Greek yogurt, mixed berries, and granola.
4. Drizzle with honey.
5. Serve immediately.

Calories: approximately 250 calories per serving.

Veggie and Egg Breakfast Sandwich

Ingredients:

- 2 whole-grain English muffins
- 1 tsp olive oil
- 2 eggs
- 2 tbsp shredded cheese
- Salt and pepper to taste
- Sliced tomato, avocado, and spinach for serving

Instructions:

1. Toast the English muffins until golden.
2. In a non-stick skillet, heat the olive oil over medium heat.
3. Crack the eggs into the skillet and cook to desired doneness (sunny side up, over-easy, etc.).
4. Place the cooked eggs on top of one half of the toasted English muffins.
5. Top with shredded cheese, salt, and pepper.
6. Add sliced tomato, avocado, and spinach.
7. Cover with the other half of the toasted English muffins to form the sandwich.

Calories: approximately 250 calories per serving.

Banana Almond Butter Toast

Ingredients:

- 2 slices of whole-grain bread
- 2 tbsp almond butter
- 1 ripe banana, sliced
- 1 tbsp honey
- 1/4 tsp cinnamon

Instructions:

1. Toast the bread slices until golden.
2. Spread almond butter on each slice of toast.
3. Top with sliced banana.
4. Drizzle with honey and sprinkle with cinnamon.
5. Serve immediately.

Calories: approximately 250 calories per serving.

Oatmeal Berry Bowl

Ingredients:

- 1 cup rolled oats
- 1 cup almond milk
- 1/2 tsp vanilla extract
- 1 tsp honey
- 1/2 cup mixed berries (strawberries, blueberries, raspberries, etc.)
- 2 tbsp chopped nuts (walnuts, almonds, pecans, etc.)

Instructions:

1. In a medium saucepan, combine the oats, almond milk, vanilla extract, and honey.
2. Cook over medium heat, stirring occasionally, until the oatmeal is soft and creamy, about 5 minutes.
3. Pour the oatmeal into a bowl.
4. Top with mixed berries and chopped nuts.
5. Serve immediately.

Calories: approximately 250 calories per serving.

Avocado Toast with Fried Egg

Ingredients:

- 2 slices of whole-grain bread
- 1 ripe avocado, mashed
- Salt and pepper to taste
- 1 tsp olive oil
- 1 egg
- Sliced tomato and red pepper flakes for serving (optional)

Instructions:

1. Toast the bread slices until golden.
2. Spread mashed avocado on each slice of toast.
3. Sprinkle with salt and pepper.
4. In a non-stick skillet, heat the olive oil over medium heat.
5. Crack the egg into the skillet and cook to desired doneness (sunny side up, over-easy, etc.).
6. Place the fried egg on top of the avocado toast.
7. Serve with sliced tomato and a sprinkle of red pepper flakes, if desired.

Calories: approximately 250 calories per serving.

Peanut Butter Banana Smoothie

Ingredients:

- 1 ripe banana
- 1/2 cup almond milk
- 1 tbsp peanut butter
- 1 tsp honey
- 1/4 tsp cinnamon
- 3-4 ice cubes

Instructions:

1. In a blender, combine the banana, almond milk, peanut butter, honey, cinnamon, and ice cubes.
2. Blend until smooth.
3. Pour into a glass and serve immediately.

Calories: approximately 250 calories per serving.

Cottage Cheese and Fruit Bowl

Ingredients:

- 1 cup cottage cheese
- 1 cup mixed fruit (strawberries, blueberries, peaches, etc.)
- 2 tbsp chopped nuts (walnuts, almonds, pecans, etc.)
- 1 tbsp honey
- 1/4 tsp cinnamon

Instructions:

1. In a bowl, combine the cottage cheese, mixed fruit, and chopped nuts.
2. Drizzle with honey and sprinkle with cinnamon.
3. Serve immediately.

Calories: approximately 250 calories per serving.

Frittata with Veggies

Ingredients:

- 1 tsp olive oil
- 1/2 cup diced onion
- 1/2 cup diced bell pepper
- 1/2 cup diced tomato
- 4 eggs
- Salt and pepper to taste
- 2 tbsp shredded cheese

Instructions:

1. In a non-stick skillet, heat the olive oil over medium heat.
2. Add the onion, bell pepper, and tomato. Cook until softened, about 5 minutes.
3. In a bowl, beat the eggs with salt and pepper.
4. Pour the beaten eggs over the veggies in the skillet.
5. Cook until the edges start to set, then sprinkle the shredded cheese over the top.
6. Finish cooking until the cheese is melted and the eggs are fully set, about 5 minutes.
7. Serve immediately.

Calories: approximately 250 calories per serving.

Ingredients:

- 1 cup Greek yogurt
- 1 cup mixed berries (strawberries, blueberries, raspberries, etc.)
- 2 tbsp granola
- 1 tsp honey

Instructions:

1. In a glass or bowl, layer the Greek yogurt, mixed berries, granola, and honey.
2. Repeat the layers until all ingredients are used.
3. Serve immediately.

Calories: approximately 250 calories per serving.

Whole-Grain Pancakes with Fresh Fruit

Ingredients:

- 1 cup whole-grain flour
- 1 tbsp sugar
- 1 tsp baking powder
- 1/4 tsp salt
- 1 cup almond milk
- 1 egg
- 1 tsp vanilla extract
- 1 cup mixed fruit (strawberries, blueberries, peaches, etc.)
- 1 tbsp maple syrup

Instructions:

1. In a large bowl, whisk together the flour, sugar, baking powder, and salt.
2. In a separate bowl, whisk together the almond milk, egg, and vanilla extract.
3. Pour the wet ingredients into the dry ingredients and stir until just combined.
4. Heat a non-stick griddle or skillet over medium heat.
5. Pour 1/4 cup batter onto the griddle for each pancake. Cook until bubbles form on the surface, then flip and cook until the other side is golden brown.

Calories: approximately 250 calories per serving.

Avocado Toast with Poached Egg

Ingredients:

- 2 slices whole-grain bread
- 1 ripe avocado
- Salt and pepper to taste
- 2 eggs
- Vinegar

Instructions:

1. Toast the bread to desired crispness.
2. Mash the avocado with salt and pepper in a bowl.
3. Spread the mashed avocado on the toast.
4. Fill a saucepan with water and bring to a simmer.
5. Add a splash of vinegar to the water.
6. Crack each egg into a small bowl or ramekin.
7. Gently slide the eggs one by one into the simmering water.
8. Cook for 3-4 minutes or until the whites are set but the yolks are still runny.
9. Use a slotted spoon to remove the eggs from the water and place on top of the avocado toast.
10. Serve immediately.

Calories: approximately 250 calories per serving.

Oatmeal with Nuts and Fresh Fruit

Ingredients:

- 1/2 cup rolled oats
- 1 cup water or almond milk
- Salt to taste
- 2 tbsp chopped nuts (walnuts, almonds, pecans, etc.)
- 1 tbsp honey
- 1 cup mixed fruit (strawberries, blueberries, peaches, etc.)

Instructions:

1. In a saucepan, bring the oats, water or almond milk, and a pinch of salt to a boil.
2. Reduce heat and simmer for 5-7 minutes or until the oats are tender.
3. Stir in the chopped nuts and honey.
4. Serve the oatmeal in a bowl topped with mixed fruit.

Calories: approximately 250 calories per serving.

Scrambled Eggs with Whole-Grain Toast

Ingredients:

- 2 eggs
- Salt and pepper to taste
- 2 slices whole-grain bread
- Butter or oil

Instructions:

1. Crack the eggs into a bowl and whisk with salt and pepper.
2. Toast the bread to desired crispness.
3. Heat a non-stick skillet over medium heat and add a little butter or oil.
4. Pour the eggs into the skillet and stir constantly until cooked to your liking.
5. Serve the scrambled eggs with the whole-grain toast.

Calories: approximately 250 calories per serving.

Peanut Butter and Banana Smoothie

Ingredients:

- 1 banana
- 1 cup almond milk
- 2 tbsp peanut butter
- 1 tsp honey
- Ice (optional)

Instructions:

1. Blend all ingredients in a blender until smooth.
2. If desired, add a few ice cubes for a thicker consistency.
3. Serve immediately.

Calories: approximately 250 calories per serving.

Yogurt Parfait with Berries and Granola

Ingredients:

- 1 cup plain Greek yogurt
- 1/2 cup mixed berries (strawberries, blueberries, raspberries, etc.)
- 1/4 cup granola
- 1 tbsp honey

Instructions:

1. In a clear glass or bowl, layer the yogurt, mixed berries, and granola.
2. Repeat until all ingredients are used up.
3. Drizzle with honey.
4. Serve immediately.

Calories: approximately 250 calories per serving.

Veggie and Cheese Omelette

Ingredients:

- 2 eggs
- Salt and pepper to taste
- 1/4 cup diced vegetables (bell peppers, onions, mushrooms, etc.)
- 1 tbsp grated cheese (cheddar, feta, etc.)
- Butter or oil

Instructions:

1. Crack the eggs into a bowl and whisk with salt and pepper.
2. Heat a non-stick skillet over medium heat and add a little butter or oil.
3. Add the diced vegetables to the skillet and cook until tender.
4. Pour the eggs over the vegetables in the skillet.
5. Sprinkle the grated cheese over the eggs.
6. Use a spatula to fold the omelette in half and cook until set.
7. Serve immediately.

Calories: approximately 250 calories per serving.

Avocado Toast with Egg

Ingredients:

- 2 slices whole-grain bread
- 1 avocado
- Salt and pepper to taste
- 1 egg
- Butter or oil

Instructions:

1. Toast the bread to desired crispness.
2. Mash the avocado and spread it over the toast.
3. Season with salt and pepper to taste.
4. Heat a non-stick skillet over medium heat and add a little butter or oil.
5. Crack the egg into the skillet and cook until the white is set and the yolk is still runny.
6. Place the egg on top of the avocado toast.
7. Serve immediately.

Calories: approximately 250 calories per serving.

Peanut Butter and Jelly Oatmeal

Ingredients:

- 1/2 cup quick-cooking oats
- 1 cup water
- 1 tbsp peanut butter
- 1 tbsp jelly
- Salt to taste

Instructions:

1. In a small saucepan, bring the water to a boil.
2. Stir in the oats, salt, and peanut butter.
3. Cook, stirring frequently, for about 2 minutes, or until the oats are soft and the mixture is creamy.
4. Remove from heat and stir in the jelly.
5. Serve immediately.

Calories: approximately 250 calories per serving.

Blueberry and Almond Butter Smoothie

Ingredients:

- 1 banana
- 1 cup frozen blueberries
- 1/2 cup plain Greek yogurt
- 1/4 cup almond milk
- 1 tbsp almond butter

Instructions:

1. Add the banana, blueberries, yogurt, almond milk, and almond butter to a blender.
2. Blend until smooth and creamy.
3. Pour into a glass and serve immediately.

Calories: approximately 250 calories per serving.

Whole Grain Pancakes with Fresh Fruit

Ingredients:

- 1 cup whole-grain flour
- 2 tsp baking powder
- 1 tbsp sugar
- 1 egg
- 1 cup almond milk
- 1 tbsp vegetable oil
- 1 cup mixed fresh fruit (strawberries, blueberries, etc.)

Instructions:

1. In a large mixing bowl, whisk together the flour, baking powder, and sugar.
2. In a separate bowl, beat together the egg, almond milk, and vegetable oil.
3. Add the wet ingredients to the dry ingredients and stir until just combined.
4. Heat a non-stick griddle or skillet over medium heat.
5. Use a 1/4 cup measure to pour the batter onto the griddle.
6. Cook until the pancakes are golden brown and bubbly on top, then flip and cook the other side.
7. Serve the pancakes hot with fresh fruit on top.

Calories: approximately 250 calories per serving.

Yogurt Parfait with Granola and Fresh Berries

Ingredients:

- 1 cup plain Greek yogurt
- 1/4 cup granola
- 1/2 cup mixed fresh berries (strawberries, blueberries, raspberries, etc.)

Instructions:

1. In a tall glass, layer half of the yogurt, then half of the granola, then half of the berries.
2. Repeat the layers one more time.
3. Serve immediately and enjoy.

Calories: approximately 200 calories per serving.

Appetizer

Caprese Skewers

Ingredients:

- 8 cherry tomatoes
- 8 fresh basil leaves
- 8 small fresh mozzarella balls
- 1 tbsp. balsamic glaze
- Salt and pepper to taste

Instructions:

1. Preheat grill or oven to 400°F (200°C).
2. Thread one cherry tomato, one basil leaf, and one mozzarella ball onto each skewer.
3. Place the skewers on a baking sheet and brush with balsamic glaze.
4. Sprinkle with salt and pepper.
5. Grill or bake for 5-7 minutes, or until the mozzarella is melted and the tomato is slightly charred.
6. Serve hot and enjoy!

Each skewer is approximately 50 calories.

Grilled Vegetable Platter

Ingredients:

- 1 medium zucchini, sliced
- 1 medium eggplant, sliced
- 1 red bell pepper, sliced
- 1 yellow bell pepper, sliced
- 1 small red onion, sliced
- 2 tbsp. olive oil
- Salt and pepper to taste

Instructions:

1. Preheat grill to medium-high heat.
2. In a large bowl, mix together the zucchini, eggplant, bell peppers, red onion, olive oil, salt, and pepper.
3. Place the vegetables on the grill and cook for 4-5 minutes on each side, or until slightly charred and tender.
4. Serve the grilled vegetables on a platter with a side of low-fat ranch dressing or hummus for dipping.

Each serving is approximately 200 calories.

Avocado and Shrimp Cocktail

Ingredients:

- 8 oz. cooked and peeled shrimp
- 2 ripe avocados, diced
- 1 small lime, juiced
- 1 tsp. diced red onion
- 1 tsp. diced cilantro
- Salt and pepper to taste

Instructions:

1. In a large bowl, combine the cooked shrimp, diced avocado, lime juice, red onion, cilantro, salt, and pepper.
2. Mix well and divide into 4 portions.
3. Serve each portion in a martini glass or on a small plate, garnished with additional cilantro and a lime wedge.

Each serving is approximately 200 calories.

Spiced Roasted Chickpeas

Ingredients:

- 1 can (15 oz) chickpeas, drained and rinsed
- 1 tbsp. olive oil
- 1 tsp. paprika
- 1 tsp. cumin
- Salt and pepper to taste

Instructions:

1. Preheat oven to 400°F (200°C).
2. Line a baking sheet with parchment paper.
3. In a medium bowl, mix together the chickpeas, olive oil, paprika, cumin, salt, and pepper.
4. Spread the chickpeas in a single layer on the prepared baking sheet.
5. Bake for 20-25 minutes, or until crispy and golden brown.
6. Serve warm or at room temperature as a snack or appetizer.

Each serving (1/4 of recipe) is approximately 150 calories.

Tomato and Feta Stuffed Mini Peppers

Ingredients:

- 12 mini sweet peppers
- 1 cup cherry tomatoes, diced
- 1/2 cup crumbled feta cheese
- 1/4 cup diced red onion
- 1 tbsp. balsamic vinegar
- Salt and pepper to taste

Instructions:

1. Preheat oven to 400°F (200°C).
2. Line a baking sheet with parchment paper.
3. Cut the tops off the mini peppers and remove the seeds.
4. In a medium bowl, mix together the cherry tomatoes, feta cheese, red onion, balsamic vinegar, salt, and pepper.
5. Fill each pepper with the tomato and feta mixture.
6. Place the peppers on the prepared baking sheet and bake for 15-20 minutes, or until the peppers are tender and the feta is slightly melted.
7. Serve hot or at room temperature as a snack or appetizer.

Each serving (2 stuffed mini peppers) is approximately 100 calories.

Spinach and Artichoke Dip

Ingredients:

- 1 cup frozen spinach, thawed and squeezed dry
- 1 cup marinated artichoke hearts, chopped
- 1/2 cup low-fat sour cream
- 1/2 cup low-fat mayonnaise
- 1/2 cup grated parmesan cheese
- 1 clove garlic, minced
- Salt and pepper to taste

Instructions:

1. Preheat oven to 375°F (190°C).
2. In a large bowl, mix together the spinach, artichoke hearts, sour cream, mayonnaise, parmesan cheese, garlic, salt, and pepper.
3. Transfer the mixture to an 8x8 inch baking dish.
4. Bake for 25-30 minutes, or until the dip is hot and bubbly.
5. Serve with whole grain crackers or vegetable sticks for dipping.

Each serving (1/4 of recipe) is approximately 200 calories.

Prosciutto-Wrapped Melon Balls

Ingredients:

- 1 medium cantaloupe, cut into bite-sized balls
- 8 slices prosciutto, cut in half
- Fresh mint leaves for garnish

Instructions:

1. Wrap each melon ball with a half slice of prosciutto.
2. Arrange the wrapped melon balls on a platter and garnish with mint leaves.
3. Serve chilled as a snack or appetizer.

Each serving (2 wrapped melon balls) is approximately 100 calories.

Grilled Peach and Burrata Salad

Ingredients:

- 2 ripe peaches, halved and pitted
- 2 oz. burrata cheese
- 1 cup mixed greens
- 1 tbsp. balsamic glaze
- Salt and pepper to taste

Instructions:

1. Preheat a grill to medium-high heat.
2. Brush the cut side of the peaches with a little oil and place them cut side down on the grill.
3. Grill for 2-3 minutes on each side, or until the peaches are tender and charred.
4. In a large bowl, mix together the mixed greens, salt, and pepper.
5. Divide the greens among two plates.
6. Top each plate with a grilled peach half and a piece of burrata cheese.
7. Drizzle with the balsamic glaze and serve.

Each serving (1 plate) is approximately 250 calories.

Cucumber and Avocado Bites

Ingredients:

- 1 medium cucumber, cut into 1/2 inch rounds
- 1 ripe avocado, peeled and diced
- 1 tbsp. fresh lemon juice
- Salt and pepper to taste

Instructions:

1. On each cucumber round, place a small spoonful of diced avocado.
2. Sprinkle with the lemon juice, salt, and pepper.
3. Serve chilled as a snack or appetizer.

Each serving (2 cucumber and avocado bites) is approximately 100 calories.

Tomato and Basil Bruschetta

Ingredients:

- 4 medium ripe tomatoes, chopped
- 1/4 cup fresh basil leaves, chopped
- 2 tbsp. extra-virgin olive oil
- 1 tbsp. balsamic vinegar
- Salt and pepper to taste
- 4 slices whole grain baguette, toasted
- 4 oz. fresh mozzarella cheese, thinly sliced

Instructions:

1. In a large bowl, mix together the tomatoes, basil, olive oil, balsamic vinegar, salt, and pepper.
2. Toast the baguette slices and top each slice with a slice of mozzarella cheese.
3. Spoon the tomato mixture over the mozzarella cheese.
4. Broil in the oven for 2-3 minutes, or until the cheese is melted and bubbly.
5. Serve hot as an appetizer.

Each serving (1 bruschetta) is approximately 250 calories.

Grilled Zucchini Roll-Ups

Ingredients:

- 2 medium zucchinis, sliced lengthwise into 1/4 inch thick strips
- 4 oz. low-fat cream cheese
- 1/4 cup grated parmesan cheese
- 1 clove garlic, minced
- Salt and pepper to taste
- Fresh basil leaves for garnish

Instructions:

1. Preheat a grill to medium-high heat.
2. In a small bowl, mix together the cream cheese, parmesan cheese, garlic, salt, and pepper.
3. Spread a small spoonful of the cream cheese mixture on each zucchini slice.
4. Roll up the zucchini slices and secure with toothpicks.
5. Place the roll-ups on the grill and cook for 2-3 minutes on each side, or until the zucchini is tender and charred.
6. Remove the toothpicks and garnish with basil leaves.
7. Serve hot as an appetizer.

Each serving (2 roll-ups) is approximately 150 calories.

Antipasto Skewers

Ingredients:

- 1 red bell pepper, cut into 1 inch squares
- 1 yellow bell pepper, cut into 1 inch squares
- 1 cup cherry tomatoes
- 1 cup fresh mozzarella balls
- 1/2 cup pitted kalamata olives
- 1/4 cup extra-virgin olive oil
- 1 tsp. dried oregano
- Salt and pepper to taste

Instructions:

1. Alternate the red and yellow bell pepper squares, cherry tomatoes, mozzarella balls, and olives on 8 skewers.
2. In a small bowl, mix together the olive oil, oregano, salt, and pepper.
3. Brush the skewers with the olive oil mixture.
4. Preheat a grill to medium-high heat and cook the skewers for 8-10 minutes, or until the vegetables are tender and charred.
5. Serve hot as an appetizer.

Each serving (2 skewers) is approximately 250 calories.

Ingredients:

- 1 large beefsteak tomato, sliced into 1/4 inch rounds
- 1 ripe avocado, peeled and sliced into 1/4 inch rounds
- 1 cup fresh basil leaves
- 8 oz. fresh mozzarella cheese, sliced into 1/4 inch rounds
- 1 tbsp. balsamic glaze
- Salt and pepper to taste

Instructions:

1. On each of 4 plates, layer a slice of tomato, a slice of avocado, a few basil leaves, and a slice of mozzarella cheese.
2. Repeat the layers until you've used all the ingredients.
3. Drizzle with the balsamic glaze and sprinkle with salt and pepper.
4. Serve chilled as an appetizer.

Each serving (1 stack) is approximately 250 calories.

Ingredients:

- 2 medium zucchinis, sliced into 1/4 inch rounds
- 1/4 cup part-skim ricotta cheese
- 1/4 cup grated Parmesan cheese
- 1 tsp. chopped fresh basil
- Salt and pepper to taste
- 1 tbsp. olive oil

Instructions:

1. In a small bowl, mix together the ricotta cheese, Parmesan cheese, basil, salt, and pepper.
2. Spread a small amount of the ricotta mixture onto each zucchini round.
3. Roll up the zucchini rounds and secure with a toothpick.
4. Brush the zucchini rolls with the olive oil.
5. Preheat a grill to medium-high heat and cook the zucchini rolls for 8-10 minutes, or until the zucchini is tender and charred.
6. Serve hot as an appetizer.

Each serving (2 rolls) is approximately 200 calories.

Prosciutto-Wrapped Melon

Ingredients:

- 1 large cantaloupe, cut into 1 inch cubes
- 8 oz. prosciutto, sliced into thin strips
- 1/4 cup chopped fresh basil
- Salt and pepper to taste

Instructions:

1. Wrap each cantaloupe cube with a strip of prosciutto.
2. Sprinkle with the basil, salt, and pepper.
3. Serve chilled as an appetizer.

Each serving (2 wrapped melon pieces) is approximately 200 calories.

Cucumber and Feta Bites

Ingredients:

- 2 large cucumbers, sliced into rounds
- 1/2 cup crumbled feta cheese
- 1/4 cup chopped fresh mint
- 1 tbsp. lemon juice
- Salt and pepper to taste

Instructions:

1. Top each cucumber slice with a small amount of feta cheese.
2. Sprinkle with the mint, lemon juice, salt, and pepper.
3. Serve chilled as an appetizer.

Each serving (4 cucumber slices) is approximately 100 calories.

Roasted Red Pepper and Goat Cheese Crostini

Ingredients:

- 8 slices of whole grain baguette
- 1/4 cup extra-virgin olive oil
- 1 large red pepper, roasted and chopped
- 4 oz. goat cheese
- Salt and pepper to taste

Instructions:

1. Preheat the oven to 375°F.
2. Brush the baguette slices with the olive oil.
3. Toast the baguette slices in the oven for 10 minutes, or until they are crisp and golden.
4. Spread a small amount of the roasted red pepper onto each baguette slice.
5. Top each slice with a dollop of goat cheese.
6. Sprinkle with salt and pepper.
7. Serve warm as an appetizer.

Each serving (2 crostini) is approximately 200 calories.

Ingredients:

- 1 lb. cooked, peeled and deveined shrimp
- 2 ripe avocados, diced
- 1/4 cup diced red onion
- 2 tbsp. freshly squeezed lemon juice
- Salt and pepper to taste

Instructions:

1. In a medium bowl, mix together the shrimp, avocados, red onion, lemon juice, salt, and pepper.
2. Serve chilled as an appetizer with crackers or toasted bread.

Each serving (1/2 cup) is approximately 200 calories.

Grilled Tomato and Mozzarella Stacks

Ingredients:

- 2 large ripe tomatoes, sliced
- 8 oz. fresh mozzarella cheese, sliced
- 2 tbsp. balsamic glaze
- Salt and pepper to taste

Instructions:

1. Preheat the grill to medium heat.
2. Alternate the tomato and mozzarella slices on skewer sticks, creating stacks.
3. Brush the stacks with the balsamic glaze.
4. Grill the stacks for 5-7 minutes, or until the cheese is melted and the tomatoes are tender.
5. Serve warm as an appetizer.

Each serving (2 stacks) is approximately 200 calories.

Grilled Eggplant and Feta Stacks

Ingredients:

- 1 large eggplant, sliced
- 4 oz. crumbled feta cheese
- 2 tbsp. chopped fresh mint
- Salt and pepper to taste

Instructions:

1. Preheat the grill to medium heat.
2. Alternate the eggplant and feta cheese slices on skewer sticks, creating stacks.
3. Sprinkle the stacks with the mint, salt, and pepper.
4. Grill the stacks for 5-7 minutes, or until the eggplant is tender and the feta cheese is slightly melted.
5. Serve warm as an appetizer.

Each serving (2 stacks) is approximately 150 calories.

Grilled Peach and Prosciutto Skewers

Ingredients:

- 4 ripe peaches, pitted and sliced
- 8 slices prosciutto
- 2 tbsp. balsamic glaze

Instructions:

1. Preheat the grill to medium heat.
2. Alternate the peach slices and prosciutto on skewer sticks.
3. Brush the skewers with the balsamic glaze.
4. Grill the skewers for 5-7 minutes, or until the prosciutto is slightly crispy and the peaches are tender.
5. Serve warm as an appetizer.

Each serving (2 skewers) is approximately 200 calories.

Stuffed Mushroom Caps

Ingredients:

- 12 medium-sized cremini mushrooms, stems removed
- 1/2 cup of chopped spinach
- 1/4 cup of grated Parmesan cheese
- 1 clove of garlic, minced
- 1 tbsp olive oil
- Salt and pepper to taste

Instructions:

1. Preheat the oven to 400°F.
2. In a bowl, mix together the chopped spinach, Parmesan cheese, minced garlic, olive oil, salt, and pepper.
3. Stuff each mushroom cap with the mixture.
4. Arrange the mushrooms on a baking sheet lined with parchment paper.
5. Bake for 15-20 minutes, or until the mushrooms are tender and the filling is golden.

Calories: approximately 100 calories per serving (based on 2 stuffed mushroom caps).

Spinach and Feta Stuffed Cherry Tomatoes

Ingredients:

- 12 cherry tomatoes, halved
- 1/2 cup of chopped spinach
- 1/4 cup of crumbled feta cheese
- 1 clove of garlic, minced
- 1 tbsp olive oil
- Salt and pepper to taste

Instructions:

1. Preheat the oven to 400°F.
2. In a bowl, mix together the chopped spinach, crumbled feta cheese, minced garlic, olive oil, salt, and pepper.
3. Spoon the mixture into the cherry tomato halves.
4. Arrange the tomatoes on a baking sheet lined with parchment paper.
5. Bake for 15-20 minutes, or until the tomatoes are soft and the filling is golden.

Calories: approximately 75 calories per serving (based on 2 stuffed cherry tomatoes).

Ingredients:

- 1 lb cooked shrimp, peeled and deveined
- 1 avocado, diced
- 2 tbsp fresh lime juice
- 2 tbsp fresh cilantro, chopped
- Salt and pepper to taste
- Cocktail sauce for serving

Instructions:

1. In a large bowl, combine the cooked shrimp, diced avocado, lime juice, cilantro, salt, and pepper.
2. Stir to mix well.
3. Serve the shrimp mixture in individual glasses with a dollop of cocktail sauce on top.

Calories: approximately 200 calories per serving (based on 4 oz cooked shrimp and 1/4 avocado).

Ingredients:

- 1 cup plain Greek yogurt
- 1 medium-sized cucumber, peeled and grated
- 1 clove of garlic, minced
- 2 tbsp fresh lemon juice
- Salt and pepper to taste
- Fresh dill for garnish

Instructions:

1. In a medium bowl, mix together the Greek yogurt, grated cucumber, minced garlic, lemon juice, salt, and pepper.
2. Stir to mix well.
3. Transfer the dip to a serving bowl and garnish with fresh dill.
4. Serve with cut-up veggies or pita chips for dipping.

Calories: approximately 70 calories per serving (based on 2 tbsp of the dip).

Grilled Peach and Burrata Salad

Ingredients:

- 2 ripe peaches, halved and pitted
- 4 oz burrata cheese
- 2 tbsp balsamic glaze
- 2 tbsp extra-virgin olive oil
- Salt and pepper to taste
- Arugula for serving

Instructions:

1. Heat a grill pan over medium-high heat.
2. Brush the peach halves with olive oil and season with salt and pepper.
3. Grill the peaches for 3-4 minutes on each side, or until grill marks appear and the peaches are tender.
4. Arrange the grilled peaches on a platter and top with the burrata cheese.
5. Drizzle with balsamic glaze and extra-virgin olive oil.
6. Serve with a handful of arugula on the side.

Calories: approximately 250 calories per serving (based on 2 grilled peach halves and 2 oz burrata cheese).

Roasted Red Pepper and Feta Crostini

Ingredients:

- 8 slices of baguette
- 1 large red pepper, roasted and sliced
- 4 oz feta cheese, crumbled
- 2 tbsp extra-virgin olive oil
- Salt and pepper to taste

Instructions:

1. Preheat the oven to 400°F.
2. Arrange the slices of baguette on a baking sheet lined with parchment paper.
3. Brush the slices with olive oil and season with salt and pepper.
4. Bake for 8-10 minutes, or until the crostini are crispy and golden.
5. Top each crostini with a slice of roasted red pepper and a sprinkle of crumbled feta cheese.
6. Serve immediately.

Calories: approximately 200 calories per serving (based on 2 crostini).

Lunch

Grilled Chicken Salad

Ingredients:

- 4 ounces of grilled chicken breast, sliced
- 2 cups mixed greens
- 1/2 cup cherry tomatoes, halved
- 1/4 cup sliced cucumber
- 1/4 cup sliced red onion
- 2 tablespoons balsamic vinaigrette

Instructions:

1. In a large bowl, combine the mixed greens, cherry tomatoes, cucumber, and red onion.
2. Toss with the balsamic vinaigrette.
3. Top with the grilled chicken breast slices.
4. Serve and enjoy.

Calories: approximately 300 calories per serving.

Veggie and Hummus Wrap

Ingredients:

- 1 large whole grain tortilla
- 2 tablespoons hummus
- 1/2 cup sliced bell peppers
- 1/2 cup sliced cucumber
- 1/4 cup shredded carrots
- 2 tablespoons tahini sauce

Instructions:

1. Spread the hummus over the whole grain tortilla.
2. Add the sliced bell peppers, cucumber, and shredded carrots.
3. Drizzle with tahini sauce.
4. Roll the wrap tightly and cut in half.
5. Serve and enjoy.

Calories: approximately 200 calories per serving.

Turkey and Avocado Sandwich

Ingredients:

- 2 slices of whole grain bread
- 4 ounces of sliced turkey
- 1/2 avocado, mashed
- 1 tomato, sliced
- 1/4 red onion, sliced
- 1/2 teaspoon of olive oil
- Salt and pepper to taste

Instructions:

1. Toast the two slices of whole grain bread.
2. Spread the mashed avocado on one slice of bread.
3. Add the sliced turkey, tomato, and red onion.
4. Drizzle with olive oil and sprinkle with salt and pepper.
5. Close the sandwich with the other slice of bread.
6. Serve and enjoy.

Calories: approximately 350 calories per serving.

Quinoa and Vegetable Bowl

Ingredients:

- 1 cup cooked quinoa
- 1 cup of mixed vegetables (such as cherry tomatoes, bell peppers, and kale)
- 2 tablespoons of lemon juice
- 1 tablespoon of olive oil
- Salt and pepper to taste

Instructions:

1. In a large bowl, mix together the cooked quinoa, mixed vegetables, lemon juice, olive oil, salt, and pepper.
2. Serve and enjoy.

Calories: approximately 350 calories per serving.

Tuna Salad Lettuce Wraps

Ingredients:

- 2 cans of tuna, drained
- 1/4 cup of diced celery
- 1/4 cup of diced red onion
- 1/4 cup of mayonnaise
- 1 tablespoon of dijon mustard
- Salt and pepper to taste
- 6 leaves of lettuce

Instructions:

1. In a large bowl, mix together the tuna, celery, red onion, mayonnaise, dijon mustard, salt, and pepper.
2. Spoon the tuna salad onto a lettuce leaf.
3. Roll the lettuce leaf around the tuna salad to form a wrap.
4. Repeat the process with the remaining lettuce leaves and tuna salad.
5. Serve and enjoy.

Calories: approximately 350 calories per serving.

Grilled Chicken and Vegetable Skewers

Ingredients:

- 1 pound of boneless, skinless chicken breast, cut into 1-inch cubes
- 2 bell peppers, cut into 1-inch squares
- 1 large onion, cut into 1-inch squares
- 1 zucchini, sliced
- 1 teaspoon of dried basil
- 1 teaspoon of dried thyme
- 1/4 cup of olive oil
- Salt and pepper to taste

Instructions:

1. Preheat the grill to high heat.
2. On 8-10 skewers, alternate the chicken cubes, bell peppers, onion, and zucchini.
3. In a small bowl, mix together the dried basil, thyme, olive oil, salt, and pepper.
4. Brush the mixture onto the skewers.
5. Place the skewers on the grill and cook for 10-12 minutes, turning occasionally, until the chicken is cooked through and the vegetables are tender.
6. Serve and enjoy.

Calories: approximately 350 calories per serving.

Grilled Vegetable and Feta Salad

Ingredients:

- 1 eggplant, sliced
- 2 bell peppers, sliced
- 1 large zucchini, sliced
- 1 red onion, sliced
- 1/4 cup of crumbled feta cheese
- 1/4 cup of balsamic vinaigrette
- Salt and pepper to taste

Instructions:

1. Preheat the grill to high heat.
2. Place the eggplant, bell peppers, zucchini, and red onion on the grill and cook for 5-7 minutes, turning occasionally, until the vegetables are tender.
3. In a large bowl, mix together the grilled vegetables, feta cheese, balsamic vinaigrette, salt, and pepper.
4. Serve and enjoy.

Calories: approximately 300 calories per serving.

Turkey, Avocado, and Cheddar Sandwich

Ingredients:

- 2 slices of whole grain bread
- 4 ounces of sliced turkey breast
- 1 avocado, mashed
- 1 slice of cheddar cheese
- Salt and pepper to taste
- A few lettuce leaves

Instructions:

1. Toast the bread.
2. Spread the mashed avocado onto one slice of bread.
3. Layer the turkey, cheddar cheese, lettuce, salt, and pepper on top of the avocado.
4. Close the sandwich with the other slice of bread.
5. Serve and enjoy.

Calories: approximately 400 calories per serving.

Chickpea and Vegetable Wrap

Ingredients:

- 1 large whole wheat wrap
- 1 can of chickpeas, drained and rinsed
- 1/2 red bell pepper, chopped
- 1/2 yellow onion, chopped
- 1/2 cup of cherry tomatoes, halved
- 1/4 cup of tahini sauce
- Salt and pepper to taste

Instructions:

1. In a large bowl, mix together the chickpeas, bell pepper, onion, cherry tomatoes, tahini sauce, salt, and pepper.
2. Place the mixture onto the center of the wrap.
3. Fold the sides of the wrap over the mixture and roll it up tightly.
4. Cut the wrap in half and serve.

Calories: approximately 400 calories per serving.

Tuna Salad Lettuce Cups

Ingredients:

- 2 cans of tuna, drained
- 1/2 cup of mayonnaise
- 1/2 cup of chopped celery
- 1/4 cup of chopped red onion
- 2 tablespoons of lemon juice
- Salt and pepper to taste
- 8 lettuce leaves

Instructions:

1. In a large bowl, mix together the tuna, mayonnaise, celery, red onion, lemon juice, salt, and pepper.
2. Spoon the mixture into each lettuce leaf.
3. Serve and enjoy.

Calories: approximately 300 calories per serving.

Grilled Chicken Salad

Ingredients:

- 4 boneless, skinless chicken breasts
- Salt and pepper to taste
- 1 head of lettuce, chopped
- 1/2 cup of cherry tomatoes, halved
- 1/2 cup of cucumber, sliced
- 1/4 cup of crumbled feta cheese
- 1/4 cup of balsamic vinaigrette

Instructions:

1. Season the chicken breasts with salt and pepper.
2. Heat a grill or grill pan to medium-high heat and grill the chicken for 4-5 minutes on each side, or until fully cooked.
3. In a large bowl, mix together the lettuce, cherry tomatoes, cucumber, feta cheese, and balsamic vinaigrette.
4. Slice the grilled chicken and add it to the salad.
5. Serve and enjoy.

Calories: approximately 450 calories per serving.

Avocado and Egg Sandwich

Ingredients:

- 2 whole grain bread slices
- 1 avocado, mashed
- 2 eggs, cooked
- Salt and pepper to taste
- 2 slices of tomato
- 2 leaves of lettuce

Instructions:

1. Spread the mashed avocado on one slice of bread.
2. Place the cooked eggs, salt, pepper, tomato, and lettuce on the other slice of bread.
3. Put the two slices of bread together to form a sandwich.
4. Cut the sandwich in half and serve.

Calories: approximately 450 calories per serving.

Grilled Chicken Salad Bowl

Ingredients:

- 4 oz grilled chicken breast, sliced
- 2 cups mixed greens
- 1/2 cup cherry tomatoes, halved
- 1/4 cup cucumber, diced
- 1/4 cup red onion, sliced
- 1 tbsp balsamic vinaigrette

Instructions:

1. In a large bowl, combine the mixed greens, cherry tomatoes, cucumber, and red onion.
2. Top with the sliced grilled chicken breast.
3. Drizzle with balsamic vinaigrette.
4. Toss to combine and serve.

Calories: approximately 400-450 calories

Veggie and Hummus Wrap

Ingredients:

- 1 whole wheat wrap
- 2 tbsp hummus
- 1 cup mixed veggies (e.g. bell peppers, carrots, cucumber)
- 1 oz feta cheese, crumbled
- Salt and pepper to taste

Instructions:

1. Spread the hummus on the wrap.
2. Top with the mixed veggies and crumbled feta cheese.
3. Sprinkle with salt and pepper.
4. Roll up the wrap and enjoy.

Calories: approximately 400-450 calories

Tuna Salad Pita

Ingredients:

- 1 whole wheat pita
- 4 oz canned tuna, drained
- 2 tbsp mayonnaise
- 1/4 cup diced celery
- 1/4 cup diced red onion
- Salt and pepper to taste

Instructions:

1. In a bowl, combine the canned tuna, mayonnaise, celery, and red onion.
2. Season with salt and pepper to taste.
3. Cut the pita in half and fill with the tuna salad.
4. Serve immediately.

Calories: approximately 400-450 calories

Quinoa and Black Bean Bowl

Ingredients:

- 1 cup cooked quinoa
- 1/2 cup cooked black beans
- 1/2 cup diced bell pepper
- 1/4 cup diced red onion
- 1 tbsp lemon juice
- Salt and pepper to taste

Instructions:

1. In a bowl, combine the cooked quinoa, black beans, bell pepper, and red onion.
2. Drizzle with lemon juice and sprinkle with salt and pepper.
3. Toss to combine and serve.

Calories: approximately 400-450 calories

Lemon and herb quinoa salad

Ingredients:

- 1 cup cooked quinoa
- 1 medium cucumber, chopped
- 1 medium tomato, chopped
- 1/2 medium red onion, chopped
- 1 lemon, juiced
- 2 tablespoons olive oil
- 1/4 teaspoon salt
- 1/4 teaspoon black pepper
- 1/4 teaspoon dried oregano
- 1/4 teaspoon dried basil

Instructions:

1. In a large bowl, mix together cooked quinoa, cucumber, tomato, and red onion.
2. In a small bowl, whisk together lemon juice, olive oil, salt, pepper, oregano, and basil.
3. Pour the dressing over the quinoa mixture and toss to combine.

Calories: 495

Tomato and Avocado Toast

Ingredients:

- 2 slices whole grain bread
- 2 ripe medium tomatoes, sliced
- 1 ripe avocado, mashed
- 1/2 lemon, juiced
- Salt and pepper, to taste
- 2 tablespoons chopped fresh cilantro

Instructions:

1. Toast bread to your desired level of crispiness.
2. Spread mashed avocado on top of each slice of toast.
3. Top each slice of toast with sliced tomatoes.
4. Squeeze lemon juice over the tomatoes and sprinkle with salt and pepper.
5. Top with chopped cilantro.

Calories: 497

Quinoa and Veggie Bowl

Ingredients:

- 1/2 cup cooked quinoa
- 1 cup mixed veggies (e.g. cherry tomatoes, bell peppers, carrots, cucumber)
- 2 tablespoons olive oil
- 1 lemon, juiced
- Salt and pepper, to taste
- 1/4 cup crumbled feta cheese
- 2 tablespoons chopped fresh parsley

Instructions:

1. Cook the quinoa according to package instructions.
2. Cut the mixed veggies into bite-sized pieces.
3. In a large bowl, mix together the cooked quinoa, veggies, olive oil, lemon juice, salt, and pepper.
4. Add the feta cheese and parsley and mix well.
5. Serve the quinoa and veggie bowl either warm or cold.

Calories: 460

Turkey Avocado Wrap

Ingredients:

- 2 whole grain tortillas
- 4 ounces sliced turkey breast
- 1 avocado, mashed
- 2 tablespoons light mayonnaise
- Salt and pepper, to taste
- 1 cup mixed greens
- 1 tomato, sliced
- 1/4 red onion, thinly sliced

Instructions:

1. Lay the tortillas flat on a cutting board.
2. Spread the mashed avocado on each tortilla.
3. Layer the turkey, mayonnaise, salt, pepper, mixed greens, tomato, and red onion on top of the avocado.
4. Roll up the tortillas tightly and slice in half.
5. Serve the turkey avocado wraps either cold or warmed in the oven for a few minutes.

Calories: 460

Tuna Salad Wrap

Ingredients:

- 100g canned tuna in water, drained
- 1 medium whole wheat tortilla
- 2 tbsp light mayonnaise
- 1 tbsp Dijon mustard
- 1 medium carrot, grated
- 1/4 small red onion, chopped
- 1 tbsp chopped fresh dill
- Salt and pepper, to taste

Instructions:

1. In a mixing bowl, combine the tuna, mayonnaise, Dijon mustard, grated carrot, chopped red onion, and chopped dill.
2. Season with salt and pepper to taste.
3. Place the mixture in the center of the tortilla, and wrap the tortilla tightly around the filling.
4. Cut the wrap in half and enjoy.

Calories 250

Tomato and Mozzarella Stuffed Avocado

Ingredients:

- 2 ripe avocados
- 4 oz fresh mozzarella cheese, diced
- 2 medium tomatoes, diced
- 2 tbsp olive oil
- 1 tbsp balsamic vinegar
- Salt and pepper, to taste

Instructions:

1. Cut the avocados in half and remove the pit.
2. In a mixing bowl, combine the diced mozzarella cheese, diced tomatoes, olive oil, balsamic vinegar, salt, and pepper.
3. Spoon the mixture into the avocado halves, filling them evenly.
4. Serve the stuffed avocados chilled and enjoy

Calories 250

Healthy Chicken Salad

Ingredients:

- 2 cooked chicken breasts, shredded (200g)
- 1 cup cherry tomatoes, halved (150g)
- 1 avocado, diced (200g)
- 1/4 cup red onion, diced (40g)
- 2 tablespoons olive oil (27g)
- 1 tablespoon lemon juice (15g)
- Salt and pepper, to taste

Instructions:

1. In a large mixing bowl, combine the shredded chicken, cherry tomatoes, avocado, and red onion.
2. In a small mixing bowl, whisk together the olive oil, lemon juice, salt, and pepper.
3. Pour the dressing over the chicken mixture and toss until evenly coated.
4. Serve the chicken salad over a bed of greens or in a sandwich.

Calories: Approximately 480 calories per serving.

Spicy Black Bean Soup

Ingredients:

- 1 tablespoon olive oil (13g)
- 1 small onion, diced (80g)
- 2 cloves garlic, minced (6g)
- 1 red bell pepper, diced (120g)
- 1 teaspoon chili powder (2g)
- 1 teaspoon cumin (2g)
- 1/2 teaspoon paprika (1g)
- 1 can black beans, drained and rinsed (240g)
- 1 cup vegetable broth (240g)
- Salt and pepper, to taste

Instructions:

1. In a large pot, heat the olive oil over medium heat.
2. Add the onion, garlic, red bell pepper, chili powder, cumin, and paprika. Cook until the vegetables are tender, about 5 minutes.
3. Stir in the black beans and vegetable broth. Bring to a boil.
4. Reduce heat and let simmer for 15 minutes.
5. Season with salt and pepper to taste.
6. Serve the soup hot with a dollop of plain Greek yogurt or a sprinkle of shredded cheese, if desired.

Calories: Approximately 460 calories per serving.

Grilled Asparagus: Ingredients:

- 1 pound asparagus
- 1 tablespoon olive oil
- Salt and pepper to taste

Instructions:

1. Preheat your grill to high heat.
2. Trim the bottom of the asparagus to remove the tough parts.
3. In a bowl, mix together the asparagus, olive oil, salt, and pepper.
4. Place the asparagus on the grill and cook for 5-7 minutes, turning occasionally, until they are slightly charred and tender.

Per serving (based on 4 servings): Cal: 107

Roasted Brussels Sprouts with Bacon

- Ingredients:

    - 1 pound brussels sprouts, trimmed and halved
    - 2 slices of bacon, chopped
    - 1 tablespoon olive oil
    - Salt and black pepper, to taste

- Directions:

1. Preheat the oven to 400°F.
2. In a large bowl, mix together the brussels sprouts, bacon, olive oil, salt, and black pepper.
3. Spread the mixture out in a single layer on a baking sheet.
4. Roast for 25-30 minutes, flipping once, until the brussels sprouts are tender and the bacon is crispy.
5. Serve as a side dish.

Calories per serving (4 servings): 191 calories

Grilled Asparagus with Parmesan Cheese

- Ingredients:

  - 1 pound asparagus, trimmed
  - 1 tablespoon olive oil
  - Salt and black pepper, to taste
  - 2 tablespoons grated parmesan cheese

- Directions:

1. Heat the grill to medium-high heat.
2. In a large bowl, mix together the asparagus, olive oil, salt, and black pepper.
3. Grill the asparagus until tender and slightly charred, about 5 minutes.
4. Sprinkle the parmesan cheese over the asparagus and serve.

Calories per serving (4 servings): 112 calories

Baked Butternut Squash with Cinnamon and Brown Sugar

- Ingredients:

  - 1 medium butternut squash, peeled and diced into 1-inch cubes
  - 1 tablespoon olive oil
  - 1 teaspoon cinnamon
  - 1 tablespoon brown sugar
  - Salt and black pepper, to taste

- Directions:

1. Preheat the oven to 400°F.
2. In a large bowl, mix together the butternut squash, olive oil, cinnamon, brown sugar, salt, and black pepper.
3. Spread the mixture out in a single layer on a baking sheet.
4. Bake for 25-30 minutes, flipping once, until the butternut squash is tender and lightly caramelized.
5. Serve as a side dish.

Calories per serving (4 servings): 140 calories

Grilled Corn on the Cob with Herb Butter

- Ingredients:

    - 4 ears of corn, husks removed
    - 1/4 cup unsalted butter, softened
    - 2 tablespoons chopped fresh herbs (such as parsley, basil, or cilantro)
    - Salt and black pepper, to taste

- Directions:

1. Heat the grill to medium-high heat.
2. In a small bowl, mix together the butter, herbs, salt, and black pepper.
3. Brush the corn with the herb butter.
4. Grill the corn until tender and slightly charred, about 10 minutes.
5. Serve as a side dish.

Calories per serving (4 servings): 158 calories

Baked Carrot Fries with Rosemary and Thyme

- Ingredients:

  - 4 medium carrots, peeled and sliced into thin fries
  - 1 tablespoon olive oil
  - 1 teaspoon dried rosemary
  - 1 teaspoon dried thyme
  - Salt and black pepper, to taste

- Directions:

1. Preheat the oven to 425°F.
2. In a large bowl, mix together the carrot fries, olive oil, rosemary, thyme, salt, and black pepper.
3. Spread the mixture out in a single layer on a baking sheet.
4. Bake for 20-25 minutes, flipping once, until the carrots are tender and slightly crispy.
5. Serve as a side dish.

Calories per serving (4 servings): 112 calories

Grilled Eggplant with Balsamic Glaze

- Ingredients:

  - 2 medium eggplants, sliced lengthwise
  - 1 tablespoon olive oil
  - Salt and black pepper, to taste
  - 1/4 cup balsamic vinegar
  - 1 tablespoon honey

- Directions:

1. Heat the grill to medium-high heat.
2. In a large bowl, mix together the eggplant, olive oil, salt, and black pepper.
3. Grill the eggplant until tender and slightly charred, about 5 minutes.
4. In a small saucepan, heat the balsamic vinegar and honey over medium heat until reduced by half.
5. Drizzle the balsamic glaze over the grilled eggplant and serve.

Calories per serving (4 servings): 128 calories

Grilled Zucchini with Lemon and Basil

- Ingredients:

    - 2 medium zucchini, sliced lengthwise
    - 1 tablespoon olive oil
    - Salt and black pepper, to taste
    - 1 lemon, juiced
    - 2 tablespoons chopped fresh basil

- Directions:

1. Heat the grill to medium-high heat.
2. In a large bowl, mix together the zucchini, olive oil, salt, and black pepper.
3. Grill the zucchini until tender and slightly charred, about 5 minutes.
4. Drizzle the lemon juice over the grilled zucchini and sprinkle with basil.
5. Serve as a side dish.

Calories per serving (4 servings): 80 calories

- Ingredients:

    - 2 medium sweet potatoes, peeled and sliced into thin fries
    - 1 tablespoon olive oil
    - 1 teaspoon paprika
    - 2 cloves garlic, minced
    - Salt and black pepper, to taste

- Directions:

1. Preheat the oven to 425°F.
2. In a large bowl, mix together the sweet potato fries, olive oil, paprika, garlic, salt, and black pepper.
3. Spread the mixture out in a single layer on a baking sheet.
4. Bake for 20-25 minutes, flipping once, until the sweet potato fries are tender and slightly crispy.
5. Serve as a side dish.

Calories per serving (4 servings): 150 calories

Roasted Broccoli with Lemon and Parmesan

- Ingredients:

    - 4 cups broccoli florets
    - 1 tablespoon olive oil
    - Salt and black pepper, to taste
    - 1 lemon, juiced
    - 1/4 cup grated parmesan cheese

- Directions:

1. Preheat the oven to 400°F.
2. In a large bowl, mix together the broccoli, olive oil, salt, and black pepper.
3. Spread the mixture out in a single layer on a baking sheet.
4. Roast for 20-25 minutes, until the broccoli is tender and slightly crispy.
5. Squeeze lemon juice over the roasted broccoli and sprinkle with parmesan cheese.
6. Serve as a side dish.

Calories per serving (4 servings): 150 calories

- Ingredients:

    - 1 bunch asparagus, trimmed
    - 1 tablespoon olive oil
    - Salt and black pepper, to taste
    - 1 lemon, juiced
    - 2 cloves garlic, minced

- Directions:

1. Heat the grill to medium-high heat.
2. In a large bowl, mix together the asparagus, olive oil, salt, and black pepper.
3. Grill the asparagus until tender and slightly charred, about 5 minutes.
4. Squeeze lemon juice over the grilled asparagus and sprinkle with garlic.
5. Serve as a side dish.

Calories per serving (4 servings): 80 calories

Baked Carrot Fries with Cumin and Cayenne Pepper

- Ingredients:

  - 4 medium carrots, peeled and sliced into thin fries
  - 1 tablespoon olive oil
  - 1 teaspoon ground cumin
  - 1/4 teaspoon cayenne pepper
  - Salt and black pepper, to taste

- Directions:

1. Preheat the oven to 425°F.
2. In a large bowl, mix together the carrot fries, olive oil, cumin, cayenne pepper, salt, and black pepper.
3. Spread the mixture out in a single layer on a baking sheet.
4. Bake for 20-25 minutes, flipping once, until the carrot fries are tender and slightly crispy.
5. Serve as a side dish.

Calories per serving (4 servings): 120 calories

- Ingredients:

    - 2 medium eggplants, sliced lengthwise
    - 1 tablespoon olive oil
    - Salt and black pepper, to taste
    - 2 tablespoons balsamic vinegar
    - 2 tablespoons chopped fresh herbs, such as basil or parsley

- Directions:

1. Heat the grill to medium-high heat.
2. In a large bowl, mix together the eggplant, olive oil, salt, and black pepper.
3. Grill the eggplant until tender and slightly charred, about 5 minutes.
4. Drizzle the balsamic vinegar over the grilled eggplant and sprinkle with fresh herbs.
5. Serve as a side dish.

Calories per serving (4 servings): 80 calories

Grilled Vegetables

Ingredients:

- 1 large eggplant, sliced
- 1 large red bell pepper, sliced
- 1 large yellow squash, sliced
- 1 large zucchini, sliced
- 1 red onion, sliced
- 1 tablespoon olive oil
- Salt and pepper to taste

Instructions:

1. Preheat grill to high heat.
2. In a bowl, mix the sliced eggplant, bell pepper, yellow squash, zucchini, and red onion with olive oil, salt, and pepper.
3. Place the vegetables on the grill and cook until they are tender and charred, about 4-5 minutes per side.
4. Serve hot.

Calories 280

Roasted Cauliflower

Ingredients:

- 1 head of cauliflower, cut into florets
- 1 tablespoon olive oil
- Salt and pepper to taste

Instructions:

1. Preheat oven to 400°F.
2. In a bowl, mix the cauliflower florets with olive oil, salt, and pepper.
3. Spread the mixture evenly on a baking sheet.
4. Roast the cauliflower for 20-25 minutes, or until tender and golden brown.
5. Serve hot.

Calories 130

Ingredients:

- 2 large sweet potatoes, peeled and sliced into fries
- 1 tablespoon olive oil
- Salt and pepper to taste

Instructions:

1. Preheat oven to 425°F.
2. In a bowl, mix the sweet potato slices with olive oil, salt, and pepper.
3. Spread the mixture evenly on a baking sheet.
4. Bake the sweet potato fries for 25-30 minutes, or until crispy and golden brown.
5. Serve hot.

Calories 230

Grilled Asparagus

Ingredients:

- 1 bunch of asparagus, trimmed
- 1 tablespoon olive oil
- Salt and pepper to taste

Instructions:

1. Preheat grill to high heat.
2. In a bowl, mix the asparagus with olive oil, salt, and pepper.
3. Place the asparagus on the grill and cook until they are tender and charred, about 4-5 minutes per side.
4. Serve hot.

Calories 90

Baked Carrot Fries

Ingredients:

- 4 medium carrots, peeled and sliced into fries
- 1 tablespoon olive oil
- Salt and pepper to taste

Instructions:

1. Preheat oven to 425°F.
2. In a bowl, mix the carrots with olive oil, salt, and pepper.
3. Spread the mixture evenly on a baking sheet.
4. Bake the carrot fries for 25-30 minutes, or until crispy and golden brown.
5. Serve hot.

Calories 150

Ingredients:

- 1 pound of Brussels sprouts, trimmed and halved
- 1 tablespoon olive oil
- Salt and pepper to taste

Instructions:

1. Preheat oven to 400°F.
2. In a bowl, mix the Brussels sprouts with olive oil, salt, and pepper.
3. Spread the mixture evenly on a baking sheet.
4. Roast the Brussels sprouts for 20-25 minutes, or until tender and golden brown.
5. Serve hot.

Calories 180

Roasted Cabbage Wedges

Ingredients:

- 1 head of green cabbage, cut into wedges
- 1 tablespoon olive oil
- Salt and pepper to taste

Instructions:

1. Preheat oven to 400°F.
2. In a bowl, mix the cabbage wedges with olive oil, salt, and pepper.
3. Spread the mixture evenly on a baking sheet.
4. Roast the cabbage wedges for 20-25 minutes, or until tender and golden brown.
5. Serve hot.

Calories 100

Ingredients:

- 1 large eggplant, sliced
- 1 tablespoon olive oil
- Salt and pepper to taste

Instructions:

1. Prehcat grill to high heat.
2. In a bowl, mix the eggplant slices with olive oil, salt, and pepper.
3. Place the eggplant on the grill and cook until they are tender and charred, about 4-5 minutes per side.
4. Serve hot.

Calories 80

Roasted Broccoli

Ingredients:

- 1 head of broccoli, cut into florets
- 1 tablespoon olive oil
- Salt and pepper to taste

Instructions:

1. Preheat oven to 400°F.
2. In a bowl, mix the broccoli florets with olive oil, salt, and pepper.
3. Spread the mixture evenly on a baking sheet.
4. Roast the broccoli for 20-25 minutes, or until tender and golden brown.
5. Serve hot.

Calories 120

Grilled Zucchini

Ingredients:

- 2 large zucchinis, sliced
- 1 tablespoon olive oil
- Salt and pepper to taste

Instructions:

1. Preheat grill to high heat.
2. In a bowl, mix the zucchini slices with olive oil, salt, and pepper.
3. Place the zucchini on the grill and cook until they are tender and charred, about 4-5 minutes per side.
4. Serve hot.

Calories 80

Dinner

Grilled Chicken Breast

Ingredients:

- 2 boneless, skinless chicken breasts
- 1 tablespoon olive oil
- Salt and pepper to taste

Instructions:

1. Preheat grill to high heat.
2. In a bowl, mix the chicken breasts with olive oil, salt, and pepper.
3. Place the chicken breasts on the grill and cook until they are fully cooked and charred, about 4-5 minutes per side.
4. Serve hot.

Calories 230

Ingredients:

- 2 tilapia fillets
- 1 tablespoon olive oil
- Salt and pepper to taste

Instructions:

1. Preheat oven to 400°F.
2. In a bowl, mix the tilapia fillets with olive oil, salt, and pepper.
3. Spread the mixture evenly on a baking sheet.
4. Bake the tilapia for 12-15 minutes, or until fully cooked and golden brown.
5. Serve hot.

Calories 230

Ingredients:

- 4 bell peppers, halved and seeded
- 1 cup cooked brown rice
- 1 can of black beans, drained and rinsed
- 1 cup of corn kernels
- 1/2 cup of salsa
- Salt and pepper to taste

Instructions:

1. Preheat oven to 375°F.
2. In a bowl, mix the brown rice, black beans, corn kernels, salsa, salt, and pepper.
3. Fill each bell pepper half with the rice and bean mixture.
4. Place the bell peppers in a baking dish and bake for 25-30 minutes, or until the peppers are tender and the filling is hot.
5. Serve hot.

Calories 220

Baked Chicken Thighs

Ingredients:

- 4 boneless, skinless chicken thighs
- 1 tablespoon olive oil
- Salt and pepper to taste
- 1 tablespoon of your favorite spice blend (optional)

Instructions:

1. Preheat oven to 400°F.
2. In a bowl, mix the chicken thighs with olive oil, salt, pepper, and your favorite spice blend (if using).
3. Spread the mixture evenly on a baking sheet.
4. Bake the chicken thighs for 25-30 minutes, or until fully cooked and golden brown.
5. Serve hot.

Calories 230

Veggie Stir-Fry

Ingredients:

- 1 tablespoon olive oil
- 1 cup sliced onion
- 1 cup sliced carrots
- 1 cup sliced bell peppers
- 1 cup sliced mushrooms
- 1 cup sliced zucchini
- Salt and pepper to taste
- 2 tablespoons soy sauce
- 1 teaspoon cornstarch (optional)

Instructions:

1. Heat the olive oil in a large pan over medium-high heat.
2. Add the onion and cook until tender, about 2-3 minutes.
3. Add the carrots and cook for an additional 2-3 minutes.
4. Add the bell peppers, mushrooms, and zucchini and cook until all the vegetables are tender, about 5-7 minutes.
5. Season the stir-fry with salt and pepper to taste.
6. If desired, thicken the stir-fry by mixing the soy sauce and cornstarch together in a small bowl and adding it to the pan. Cook until the sauce has thickened, about 1-2 minutes.
7. Serve hot over rice or noodles.

Calories 400

Ingredients:

- 4 tilapia fillets
- 1 tablespoon olive oil
- Salt and pepper to taste
- 4 large tomatoes, diced
- 1/2 cup kalamata olives, pitted and chopped
- 2 tablespoons chopped fresh basil

Instructions:

1. Preheat oven to 400°F.
2. In a bowl, mix the tilapia fillets with olive oil, salt, and pepper.
3. Spread the tilapia in a baking dish.
4. Top the tilapia with the diced tomatoes, kalamata olives, and basil.
5. Bake the tilapia for 15-20 minutes, or until fully cooked and the tomatoes are juicy and the basil is fragrant.
6. Serve hot.

Calories 230

Grilled Chicken and Vegetable Skewers

Ingredients:

- 1 pound boneless, skinless chicken breast, cut into 1-inch cubes
- 1 red bell pepper, cut into 1-inch pieces
- 1 yellow bell pepper, cut into 1-inch pieces
- 1 onion, cut into 1-inch pieces
- 1 zucchini, cut into 1-inch rounds
- Salt and pepper to taste
- 2 tablespoons olive oil

Instructions:

1. Preheat grill to medium-high heat.
2. On each skewer, alternately thread the chicken, red and yellow bell pepper, onion, and zucchini.
3. Brush the skewers with olive oil and season with salt and pepper.
4. Place the skewers on the grill and cook, turning occasionally, until the chicken is fully cooked and the vegetables are slightly charred, about 10-15 minutes.
5. Serve hot.

Calories 450

Lentil and Vegetable Soup

Ingredients:

- 2 tablespoons olive oil
- 1 onion, chopped
- 2 cloves garlic, minced
- 1 carrot, diced
- 1 celery stalk, diced
- 1 cup dried green or brown lentils, rinsed
- 4 cups vegetable broth
- 1 can diced tomatoes
- Salt and pepper to taste
- Fresh parsley for garnish (optional)

Instructions:

1. Heat the olive oil in a large pot over medium heat.
2. Add the onion and cook until tender, about 2-3 minutes.
3. Add the garlic and cook for an additional 1-2 minutes.
4. Add the carrot, celery, lentils, vegetable broth, diced tomatoes, salt, and pepper.
5. Bring the soup to a boil, then reduce heat and let it simmer until the lentils are tender, about 25-30 minutes.
6. Serve hot with fresh parsley (if desired).

Calories 300

Grilled Chicken Salad

Ingredients:

- 4 oz boneless, skinless chicken breast
- 1 cup mixed greens
- 1/4 cup cherry tomatoes, halved
- 1/4 cup cucumber, sliced
- 1 tbsp balsamic vinaigrette
- Salt and pepper to taste

Season chicken with salt and pepper. Heat a grill pan over medium-high heat and cook chicken for about 4-5 minutes per side, or until cooked through. In a large bowl, combine greens, cherry tomatoes, cucumber, and vinaigrette. Toss to combine. Top salad with grilled chicken.

Calories: approximately 300

Broiled Tilapia with Roasted Vegetables

Ingredients:

- 4 oz tilapia fillet
- 1/2 cup chopped zucchini
- 1/2 cup chopped red bell pepper
- 1/2 cup chopped yellow onion
- 1 tbsp olive oil
- Salt and pepper to taste

Preheat oven to broil. Place tilapia in a baking dish and season with salt and pepper. Broil for 4-5 minutes, or until cooked through. In a separate baking dish, toss zucchini, bell pepper, onion, olive oil, salt, and pepper. Roast for 20 minutes, or until vegetables are tender. Serve tilapia with roasted vegetables on the side.

Calories: approximately 200

Veggie Stir-Fry

Ingredients:

- 1 cup broccoli florets
- 1 cup sliced mushrooms
- 1 cup sliced bell peppers
- 1 tbsp sesame oil
- 1 clove garlic, minced
- 1 tbsp low-sodium soy sauce
- 1 tbsp cornstarch
- 1 tsp sugar

Heat a wok or large skillet over high heat. Add sesame oil, garlic, broccoli, mushrooms, and bell peppers. Stir-fry for about 4-5 minutes, or until vegetables are tender. In a small bowl, whisk together soy sauce, cornstarch, and sugar. Add to the wok and stir-fry for another 2 minutes, or until the sauce thickens. Serve with brown rice.

Calories: approximately 300

Baked Chicken Parmesan

Ingredients:

- 4 oz boneless, skinless chicken breast
- 1/4 cup Italian-seasoned breadcrumbs
- 1 tbsp grated parmesan cheese
- 1 tsp olive oil
- 1/4 cup marinara sauce
- 1 oz mozzarella cheese, shredded

Preheat oven to 400°F. In a shallow dish, combine breadcrumbs and parmesan cheese. Dip chicken into breadcrumb mixture to coat. Heat olive oil in a skillet over medium-high heat. Cook chicken for about 4-5 minutes per side, or until golden brown. Transfer chicken to a baking dish and top with marinara sauce and mozzarella cheese. Bake for 10 minutes, or until cheese is melted and bubbly.

Calories: approximately 400

Quinoa Stuffed Bell Peppers

Ingredients:

- 2 large bell peppers, halved and seeded
- 1/2 cup cooked quinoa
- 1/2 cup cooked black beans
- 1/4 cup diced onion
- 1/4 cup diced tomato
- 1 tbsp chopped cilantro
- 1 tsp chili powder
- 1 tsp cumin
- 1 tsp olive oil
- Salt and pepper to taste

Preheat oven to 375°F. In a large bowl, combine quinoa, black beans, onion, tomato, cilantro, chili powder, cumin, olive oil, salt, and pepper. Fill each pepper half with quinoa mixture. Place peppers in a baking dish and bake for 25-30 minutes, or until peppers are tender.

Calories: approximately 250 per serving

Baked Sweet Potato and Black Bean Tacos

Ingredients:

- 1 large sweet potato, peeled and diced
- 1/2 cup cooked black beans
- 1/4 cup diced red onion
- 1 tbsp olive oil
- 2 tsp chili powder
- 1 tsp cumin
- Salt and pepper to taste
- 4 corn tortillas
- 1/4 cup shredded lettuce
- 1/4 cup diced tomato
- 1 tbsp diced avocado

Preheat oven to 400°F. In a large bowl, combine sweet potato, black beans, onion, olive oil, chili powder, cumin, salt, and pepper. Spread mixture in a single layer on a baking sheet and bake for 25-30 minutes, or until sweet potato is tender. Warm tortillas in a skillet over medium heat. Fill each tortilla with sweet potato mixture, lettuce, tomato, and avocado.

Calories: approximately 400 per serving

Stuffed Portobello Mushrooms

Ingredients:

- 4 large portobello mushrooms, stemmed
- 1/2 cup cooked quinoa
- 1/2 cup diced tomatoes
- 1/4 cup diced onion
- 1 clove garlic, minced
- 1 tbsp chopped basil
- 1 tsp balsamic vinegar
- 1 tsp olive oil
- Salt and pepper to taste

Preheat oven to 400°F. In a large bowl, combine quinoa, tomatoes, onion, garlic, basil, balsamic vinegar, olive oil, salt, and pepper. Stuff each mushroom cap with quinoa mixture. Place mushrooms in a baking dish and bake for 20-25 minutes, or until mushrooms are tender.

Calories: approximately 250 per serving

Shrimp Scampi with Zucchini Noodles

Ingredients:

- 4 oz raw shrimp, peeled and deveined
- 2 medium zucchinis, spiralized
- 1 tbsp butter
- 2 cloves garlic, minced
- 1 tbsp lemon juice
- 1 tsp dried oregano
- Salt and pepper to taste

In a large skillet, melt butter over medium heat. Add garlic and cook for 1 minute, or until fragrant. Add shrimp and cook for 2-3 minutes, or until shrimp are pink and cooked through. Stir in lemon juice, oregano, salt, and pepper. Remove from heat. In a separate pan, cook zucchini noodles for 2-3 minutes, or until just tender. Serve shrimp scampi over zucchini noodles.

Calories: approximately 300 per serving

Grilled Salmon with Avocado Salsa

Ingredients:

- 4 oz salmon fillet
- 1 ripe avocado, diced
- 1/2 cup diced tomato
- 1/4 cup diced red onion
- 1 tbsp chopped cilantro
- 1 tbsp lime juice
- Salt and pepper to taste

Preheat grill to high heat. Season salmon fillet with salt and pepper. Grill for 4-5 minutes on each side, or until cooked through. In a small bowl, mix together avocado, tomato, onion, cilantro, lime juice, salt, and pepper to make salsa. Serve salmon with avocado salsa.

Calories: approximately 400 per serving

Chicken and Vegetable Stir-Fry

Ingredients:

- 4 oz boneless, skinless chicken breast, sliced
- 1 cup diced mixed vegetables (such as bell peppers, carrots, and broccoli)
- 1 tbsp olive oil
- 2 cloves garlic, minced
- 1 tbsp low-sodium soy sauce
- 1 tsp honey
- Salt and pepper to taste

In a large skillet, heat olive oil over high heat. Add chicken and cook for 2-3 minutes, or until browned on both sides. Add vegetables, garlic, soy sauce, honey, salt, and pepper to the skillet and stir-fry for another 2-3 minutes, or until vegetables are tender. Serve over brown rice.

Calories: approximately 300 per serving

Conclusion

In conclusion, this cookbook is a great resource for those looking to maintain a healthy and balanced diet. All of the recipes included contain less than 500 calories, making it easy to incorporate nutritious and delicious meals into your daily routine. Whether you're a seasoned cook or just starting out, these recipes are sure to impress and satisfy. So, grab a pan, preheat your oven, and start cooking!